Said Mouse to Mole

Copyright © QEB Publishing, Inc. 2004

Published in the United States by
QEB Publishing, Inc.
23062 La Cadena Drive
Laguna Hills
Irvine
CA 92653

Library of Congress Control Number 2004101905

ISBN 1-59566-014-3

Written by Clare Bevan
Designed by Alix Wood
Editor Hannah Ray
Illustrated by Sanja Rešček

Series Consultant Anne Faundez
Creative Director Louise Morley
Editorial Manager Jean Coppendale

Printed and bound in China

START
Reading

Said Mouse to Mole

by Clare Bevan

QEB Publishing, Inc.

Said Mouse to Mole,
"How do you do?"

Said Mole to Mouse,
"And how are you?"

Said Mouse, "I'm feeling sad and blue."

Said Mole, "I'm feeling gloomy, too."

5

Said Mouse, "I wish that I could fly,
Like Bee and Bird across the sky."

Said Mole, "But if you fly around,
I'll miss you when I'm underground."

Said Mole, "I wish that I could run,
Like Squirrel in the summer sun."

8

Said Mouse, "But if you play outside,
I'll miss you when I have to hide."

9

Said Mouse, "I wish that I could float,
Like Beetle in his sailboat."

Said Mole, "But if you sail away,
Who will talk to me all day?"

11

Said Mole, "I wish that I could sing,
Like Blackbird with his glossy wing."

12

Said Mouse, "But if you sing and shout,
The Big Bad Cat will prowl about!"

Said Mouse, "I wish that I could shine,
Like sunbeams in the summertime."

Said Mole, "But if you're shiny bright,
The Big Bad Cat will prowl all night."

Said Mole, "I wish that I could be
Taller than the tallest tree."

16

Said Mouse, "But if you grow so tall,
Your little house will be too small."

Said Mouse, "I wish that I could change
To something beautiful and strange."

Said Mole, "But if you're strange and new,
Will you like me? Will I like you?"

Said Mouse to Mole, said Mole to Mouse,
"Don't leave your home. Don't leave your house.
Don't be a snail. Don't be a star...

I LIKE YOU JUST THE WAY YOU ARE!"

What do you think?

Which animals, who can fly,
does Mouse want to be like?

Can you
remember
who floats in
a sailboat?

Mouse does not want
Mole to grow taller
than the tallest tree.
Can you remember why not?

How many animals can you spot in this picture?
What kind of animals are they?

Parents' and teachers' notes

- Read the story together and encourage your child to talk about the two friends. What are their names, and what do they look like?
- Together, look at the pictures. Talk with your child about what is happening in each one.
- Can your child think of reasons why the two friends want to be different?
- Encourage your child to say what he/she thinks of Mouse and Mole's ideas. Would your child like to be able to fly like Bird and Bee? Would he/she enjoy being like Beetle, and floating in a sailboat? Does your child think that Mouse and Mole's ideas are good ideas? Why or why not?
- Ask your child which special powers he/she would like to have.
- Talk to your child about his/her friends. What makes each of your child's friends special?

- Read the story again, pausing to let your child guess the rhymes.
- Make up some silly rhymes together, such as "I wish that I could jump/Onto a friendly camel's hump" or "I wish that I had handy/A bowlful of peppermint candy."
- Enjoy the rhythms of the story together. Clap along with the verses as you read.
- Have fun imagining what Mouse and Mole would look like if their wishes came true; for example, a mole taller than the tallest tree!
- Invent some strange creatures, such as a flying cat or a juggling elephant. Encourage your child to be as imaginative as he/she can.
- Invite your child to draw pictures of his/her imaginary animals and to describe them to you.
- Take turns finishing the sentence, "I wish I could…"